POETIC FORMS

EDITED BY JENNI HARRISON

First published in Great Britain in 2018 by:

Forward Poetry

Remus House
Coltsfoot Drive
Peterborough
PE2 9BF
Telephone: 01733 890099
Website: www.forwardpoetry.co.uk

FOREWORD

Here at Forward Poetry our aim has always been to provide a bridge to publication for unknown poets and allow their work to reach a wider audience. We believe that poetry should not be exclusive or elitist but available to be accessed and appreciated by all.

We hope you will agree that our latest collection with its combination of traditional and modern verse is one that everyone can enjoy. The poets have tackled a variety of poetic forms, from haiku to villanelle, from epistle to free verse. Whether you prefer humorous rhymes or poignant odes there is something inside these pages that will suit every reader's taste.

We are very proud to present this anthology and we are sure it will provide entertainment and inspiration for years to come.

CONTENTS

THE POEMS

END SONG

I lie here and I sink.
A gentle movement to the earth that will be me,
My pink shall drain, and only green will blanket me.

A chill breeze waves.
Dash yellows flutter in defiance.
The hand that paves will grey them all,
But not me. I sink until I'm ended.

My slick screen blackens.
Mirrored edges that now gather dust.
Though was full of light and sound.
Bracken curls and carves through broken shards of glass.

Now thinking back, sun streaks appear.
Across my deep green moors,
With mist and great tears of heather.
I fear I can't be with it again.

So I fight
No animation strikes me
Nothing will take me
I am the one who destroyed the black grasp-

Yet it laughs oh so sweetly,
And I nod oh so meekly.

Alfie Morland

FORWARD SHAMPOOING

I thought it might be just a bit of fun
To write the ultimate poem about life, the universe, everything
and everyone
But it wouldn't get accepted as it would be too long
So it'd just be a colossal waste of time, I may as well write a song
I thought it might be just a bit of fun, again
To write a poem about a boy who became a rock star at the age
of ten
And ended up surpassing Elvis Presley as regards the extent of
his fame
He didn't end up meeting with the same early grave
I thought it might be just a bit of fun
To write a poem about having my hair washed by my mum
She used to run the water in the kitchen sink
And then I leaned over and put my head in it
Scrub away, scrub away, scrub away, the SR way
(Although that's toothpaste, she didn't use to use that on my hair)
I thought it might be just a bit of fun
To write a poem about my mum having her hair washed by
her mum
You see, despite the fact that she very often was
She caught nits, which will invade your scalp even if it's always
getting washed
Her mum told her not to sit next to that boy in school
And went out and bought her a special shampoo
And I still have my late mother's long, shiny plaits
I could send them off to go towards making wigs for cancer
patients perhaps

I supposed it might not be all that bad
To write a poem about a girl having her hair washed by her dad
As I've seen that being done in a basin on TV
In an old Canadian TV series called 'Kids of Degrassi Street'
And I can recall it happening to me
On one occasion when my mum was lying in bed poorly
And this poem is different from all the rest, as you can see
In that the composition of it is really quite unique
I decided, in the end, it wasn't so bad
To write a poem about a girl having her hair washed in the swimming baths
She stood on a step at the entrance to the showers in there
And put her head down as a blob of shampoo was poured onto her hair
But I'm not going to just keep eternally waffling on
Like a long-playing record, or the uncut version of the radio edit of a song
That kind of conduct just wouldn't be the norm
For a person who's invented their own poetic form

Philip Dalton

FOR THE LOVE OF ROME

I walk alone
On the streets of Rome
Couldn't make it in the UK
So I packed my troubles and moved in May

The Italian breeze
The smell of fresh cheese
Life here is of new beginnings
Even though I felt like a gladiator
A prisoner of war, a slave for sure

Question is
Can I make it on my own?
Here in Rome
Because love sliced me deep with a scalpel
Couldn't even find answers or peace at the Sistine Chapel
So, I placed my feet in the arena
Waited to be beaten, to be put to death
This world is NO world without my soulmate

Silent spectators waited
Live or die, I debated
My name is Anna, and I'm broken you see
In past life, was I here in 1483?

'Cause if the cruelty of one's mind can battle and win
I will feast until that joyful grin
Leads me to the Trevi Fountain
There, I shall flick my coin and build a mountain
A colosseum just for you and me
In the baths of Caracalla is where we would lie

The reflections from the waters
Glittered on our faces
Through our eyes
We washed like lovers in paradise

If I'm dreaming
Then let me remain asleep
Don't take me to the mouth of truth
(La bocca Della verita)
No open mouths or wide eyes
Will tell me where you are

Deep in this coma
I will walk the Roman road
Resting by roadside tombs
I am surrounded by catacombs

This dark, ancient place wasn't made for fairies
My pain scattered across underground cemeteries
For the love of Rome
Again I ask can I make it on my own?
Speak now, as I take one last breath
And start this journey to be with you
My beautiful romance, remember it is still may
Left you a note by the Appian Way
Follow my words, return to me
Free me from this coma
Live in me, stay in Roma.

Anna Durante

TOMORROW'S CHILD

A babe asleep safe in her mother's arms,
Is unaware of life that is come
And how as years go by that life will change.
Needs nothing at this moment except love
And food and warmth its parents will provide.
That's all she knows and all she needs to know.

From infant years to school, much more she'll know
Before she's ready for another's arms,
The tools for life her teacher's will provide,
Preparing her for all that is to come.
Yet still she will enjoy her parent's love,
No matter that her life will always change.

Then teenage years arrive, a time of change.
Who is this girl her parents hardly know,
Who actively seeks out another's love?
And shuns the safety of her mother's arms.
Embraces now, the life that is to come
And all the good and bad it will provide.

Then children of her own she will provide,
Her parents help her through this time of change.
Back to the family home she often comes,
It's they who taught the values that she knows.
Her mother holds a grandchild in her arms,
Bestows on him a different kind of love.

Then comes the time her parents cannot love.
They've passed from life so cannot now provide
The warmth she felt inside their loving arms

And this, perhaps, her biggest, saddest change.
Mortality she now begins to know
And inwardly she fears what is to come.

Prepares her family now for what's to come,
They learn to nurture and they learn to love
And this is all they really need to know.
For they can each for their own family provide
And thus the world continues, does not change
As long as there are welcome, loving arms.

As generations come, each one provides,
Freely gives love and this will never change.
A family trait, known by their loving arms.

Joyce Walker

MEET TREVOR

Meet Trevor
'Ello fella'
Every night he'll polish off a crate of Stella
Trevor is ruthless
Smokes like a chimney
It's left him toothless

Apoplectic, paralytic with rage
His only tooth looks like a rusty bird cage

St Georges flag on his wheelie bin
His mind as dirty as his van

This obnoxious weasel has a bumper sticker saying
'HONK IF YOU'RE HORNY.'
His chats up lines are feudal and corny
He's scruffy and scrawny

Every Tuesday he snakes off to the local strip club
The salacious smut sees Claire's on her shift
Doing private dances for lousy tips
Trevor licks his lips, like a lion stalking its prey
Like a panting dog on a hot day

He wakes up depressed and vexed
He's £60 down and he can't remember the sex

Trevor, on a constant war path
Embodies the sin of wrath
Why does he hate life?

At school, Trevor was the lunchtime punch bag
Summer holidays flew by but school's day dragged
His subjects he was flunking, wasn't long before he was bunking
His dad was a heartless bastard
Would always come home plastered
Trevor would hide in his cupboard
His mum wasn't exactly mother Hubbard
Even now on her dying bed she says he's better off dead
That's our Trev
A donkey for the rest of his life
Carrying the weight of a troubled childhood on his back
A childhood he can't get back
Now, he's a degenerate with a short fuse
I can't see it getting any better
Can you?
Boom!

Louis Antoniou

MY HOMELAND

Roughly hexagonal, by sea and mountains,
from Gaul to Republic, you've flourished well.
A sweltering south, summer mostly bright,
a freezing north, winter brings us together.
The storming of the Bastille, what a night!
Liberté, Égalité, Fraternité; motto of the land.

Freedom captures people of the whole land.
Most cities stop at noon for sustenance. Mountains
of wine flow in bistros, cafés' terraces by night.
Moon croissants to start the day, are going well
before strolling to Eiffel, Mona Lisa; together
take our breath away. Oh, Sacré-Coeur's bright

lights illuminate the city. Along the bright
Champs Élysées, luxury colours this wonderful land,
for a journey dream, couples hop onboard together
a Bateau-Mouche over the River Seine; mountains
of experiences. An exquisite evening as well
as lovers' heart and soul pounding all night.

From the super yacht's deck, they venture by night
to the French Riviera, sighed the sun's mirror so bright
over still water. Endless beaches and coastlines well
shaped for the beauty of visitors. Oh, lucky land!
anchoring at Porquerolles; Island, take your mountain
bikes into pure paradise. No cars, a fun get-together.

So genius, Pasteur and Curie brings us together
a medical breakthrough, a better healthcare while at night

Descartes and Ronsard naturally wrote mountains
of poems. Reading them till the day dawned bright.
Vineyards spread the hexagon, connoisseur's land
to these countries, let champagne escape; then farewell!

Nicole Gilbert

GENESIS OF THE STONEHENGE

There once was a young man from Penge
Who was intrigued by the Stonehenge.
He researched history
And solved the mystery.
But first he discovered the menge.

On one stone, a face is sometimes seen.
Which is only seen when trees are green.
The stone is the architect.
He keeps the stones perfect
And has possessed one stone in-between.

Dancing giants is another myth.
They joined hands in a ring and froze forthwith.
The giants turned to stone
And did not even groan.
This is the legend which has most grith.

Stonehenge is also known as gallows.
The stones are gateways of the hallows.
This is where mankind arrives
And marks the end of their lives.
Open a gateway and horror bellows.

The stones were owned by a woman it's told.
Satan tricked the woman out of gold.
They have an evil power
Which will make you cower.
In Wiltshire, they stand in the cold.

Devil bragged none can tell how many stones.
"That is more than thee canst tell," Friar hones.
Devil threw a stone at the friar.
The friar's strength I admire.
His heel dented one of the huge stones.

The young man from the town of Penge
Travelled to the Wiltshire Stonehenge.
The stones looked very grand.
All standing hand in hand.
The young man decided to test the menge.

He climbed onto a stone that was tall.
Looking around he could see the mall.
The stone started to move.
There is nothing left to prove.
The man vanished with a thunderous squall.

Inderjeet Deusi

MESSAGE IN A BOTTLE

I keep writing all these poems,
Of a love that's lost, cannot be retrieved,
So this is a message in a bottle thrown out into the sea.
I'm unsure if this will get to you, you could be anywhere.
Still, you're not here with me sat by the shore,
Enjoying the moonlight, I so love to explore,
Sitting together, on the silken sand
holding my love-hungry hand, inside your hand,
Whispering, mysterious words you know
to make me understand the beat within my soul.
I scroll up said note,
Place it inside this glimmering glass bottle,
Press the cork in the top,
Now it's sealed, ready for travel.
I look out upon the serene night sky,
Reminiscing on the time,
I was mesmerised by those deep brown eyes.
I whisper the words,
"Please come back."
Throw the bottle from my hand,
The tide swallows my message, off it goes,
It sets sail dragged from the safety of sand,
Afloat, on its own,
Away from land.
Maybe one day you will retrieve it,
I hope in your head you don't misconceive it,
You should know it's from the heart,
So of course, I'll always protest that I mean it.

A selfless act,
Lost and maybe,
Never found,
Just a bit of paper, screwed up in a bottle,
I know right it's awful,
What a terrible debacle.

Nicki T James

THE POLITICIAN

Words like sweet honey potion
poured into their ears
sometimes soothing
sometimes feeding their fears

No cares for the electorate
he never has and never will
as long as he is consistent
considerate and moderate
his polls will only go uphill

Gaining support and winning votes
at all costs
he cares not for the rules of thumb
for his new fan base is the self-entitled
naive and wonderfully dumb

He also targets the youth
for they hold him in adoration
So righteous, moral and couth
believing every word of glorious liberation

Tension mounts as the date draws near
statistics and opinion polls feed the public fear
TV debates, interviews and papers slate
the public will soon decide his political fate

The day of the ballot comes and goes
his opposition
his enemies
are in their death throes

Now he stands jubilant
outside Ten Downing Street
smiling proudly at his masterful deceit
and hiding his murderous contempt
at those protesting beyond the gate

After his heartfelt speech worthy of a saint
and thanking his loyal supporters
off he skulks behind door number ten
rarely to be seen again
only to be remembered as Britain's cruellest tyrant

Karl Hawkins

AWAKENING

You showed me the sunshine
When I lived in the shade
You showed me the stars
On their nightly parade
You showed me the small things
That I just could not see
And you awakened the lover
That was hiding in me

You were there by my side
When I felt all alone
Your voice reassured me
I was not on my own
And I needed you there
More than I realised
You were my strength
And you stood by my side

You took control
When things seemed so wrong
I heard just noise
Whilst you heard a sweet song
What would I do
And where would I go?
You mean everything to me
And I love you so

You are brighter than diamond
I was darker than stone

You had friends all around you
Whilst I lived life alone
You were always my lady
Only you held the key
To awaken the lover
That was hiding in me

You helped me stand tall
Like I once used to be
You're my reason for living
The one girl for me
With your caring and sharing
Through life's finite days
Till the end of the rainbow
I will love you always

You helped me stand tall
Like I once used to be
And you awakened the lover
That was hiding in me.

Keith Nuhrenburg-Wilson

CLEO

We bought a dog for Christmas
As many people do.
We didn't want a big one
So we bought a small Shih Tzu.
She changed our lives completely
Though found it hard to cooperate
So we booked her in for training
Although I think we were too late.
We taught her to 'sit' and to 'stay'
But when we called her name
She totally ignored us and went her own sweet way.
In classes she was brilliant
And quickly won a star
But then forgot the lesson by the time she reached the car.
We even in despair called Google for advice.
'How do we train a Shih Tzu?' They answered in a trice.
'Don't even bother trying, they're impossible to train'.
So the money spent on lessons was completely down the drain.
She thought she was pack leader
And led us a merry dance.
Anyone want a Shih Tzu by any chance?
But a dog's not just for Christmas
So we walked her every day
And there's not enough money in the world
That would make us give her away.
She gives us love and total trust
Though obedient she's not
But she gives us joy and company
And we love her such a lot.

Pamela Matthews

I WRITE

I write...
From pain,
So I won't drown in the rain,
To release society's deepest strain,
As the world is full of leaders so vain,
Use my mind to be creative and with words infuse my brain,
Exhale from the oppression so my best self I can reclaim,
It often seems lonely as from destructive relations I abstain,
From politics and religion I refrain,
Because from voting and superhuman controlling powers what do we have to gain?
It's all a game!
To control under one world order so eventually we are all easier to be slain,
So I write from pain,
A pain which is designed by those who reign,
I see it as a journey as my subconscious am trying to train,
Working to tame,
For it is responsible for the success of our ultimate desires so towards this I aim,
As I want to reach my spiritual plain,
Taking my power back and forget about who is to blame,
To release and remove these bondages and chain,
This is my space, my domain!
This is where I rule, where I reign,
From here I experience tranquillity and attain,
My best self and maintain,
My sanity without strain.

Kadian Thomas

ON THE BANKS OF THE RIVER DEE

(A ballad)

Come, my love, let's run away,
it's time for us to leave this place.
It's dreary here; the streets are grey,
I see the sadness on your face.
Let's flee tonight and leave no trace,
our feet and hearts will wander free,
and our sorrows soon will be erased,
on the banks of the River Dee.

There, where the river gently flows
o'er pebbles and past wild flowers,
there, where the grass so golden grows,
we'll find a place to pass the hours;
a special spot that's purely ours,
where we can paddle and simply be,
in awe of the water's calming powers,
on the banks of the River Dee.

We'll gather armfuls of firewood,
as daylight fades and the mountains sigh,
and life will feel so full and good
as stars light up the infinite sky.
We'll take our wood and pile it high,
and huddle together lovingly,
as the fire burns on into the night,
on the banks of the River Dee.

And then at last we'll lay down side by side
'neath the boughs of an alder tree,
fall asleep to the sounds of the lapping tide,
on the banks of the River Dee.

Sara Collie

RED ALERT

"More floods in the north," says the man on TV,
They've issued another red alert.
More sandbags to stack across more front doors,
Desperate to hold back nature's power.

They've issued another red alert.
A few hours warning is all they can give.
Desperate to hold back nature's power;
Remembering how it was last time.

A few hours warning was all they could give;
A chance to move what they can upstairs.
Remembering how it was last time;
Knowing just what lies ahead.

A chance to move what they can upstairs,
As they nervously wait for the ominous sound.
Knowing just what lies ahead,
When the waters surge through the narrow street.

As they nervously wait for the ominous sound,
They do what they can to limit the heartache,
When the waters surge through the narrow street.
They offer a prayer to whoever will hear.

They do what they can to limit the heartache.
More sandbags to stack across more front doors.
They offer a prayer to whoever will hear.
"More floods in the north," says the man on TV.

Bryn Strudwick

THE ETERNAL DREAM

He lost his doggy in a dream,
How vivid, how real it seemed.
He searched about that 'place' of 'mind'
Through swirling mists and restless times.
Whilst other doggies by the pack
Run about freely, forwards, back.
But he saw no trace of his canine pal
Lost in a dream forever now.
He woke up in a state of sweat,
His doggy was more than just a pet,
And there he lay on the bedside rug,
Safe and sound and sleeping snug,
But now he had recurring dreams,
So real, so vivid each one seemed
Searching about that place of mind,
Through swirling mists and restless times.
Searching in vain for his doggy still,
Lost in a dream and always will.
The years swam by and age came on,
His doggy friend in life had gone,
Until one night, all tired and old
He searched his dreams and there behold
Through swirling mists of that timeless place
He once again came face-to-face
With his dearest friend he'd sought in vain.
So happy to be united again
And off they walked through haze and smoke,
In a dream from which he never awoke.

Peter Terence Ridgway

A WITCH'S TORMENT

The stones, they tell with ten and three
of life's despair or destined glee
But, woe to one whose hand they cast
for fate is one that's bound to last
A reading, oh but one's great plan
to gaze the eyes of fated man
A sign, to snuff hope's tiny glow
or hate's bright flame, to watch it grow
A woeful plea to stall time's hands
unheard, for there it stands
The life of one from dawn to dusk
laid bare, for all who trusts
A clear view of envy, tinted green
or love's sweet tingle, numb or pain
A witch will see, and perhaps tell
the soul of one inclined to sell
A life, here and soon no more
the up and down of what's in store
A seer's job, through secrets given
to read the runes of one who's bidding
The answer, hidden within the stone
is hers to tell and hers alone
But, tears they flow and fall they will
hearts they break, crush and fill
A witch's day is far from done
when stones are packed and all are gone
Happy. Hopeful. Sad. Forlorn.
A face, she'll see a year and one

Farrah Parchment

THE GARDEN

Gardening to many folk is not a chore
Hard to believe a labour of love is fun
Varied tasks await as you step out the door
Much more appealing when warm under the sun
Positive enjoyment something to adore
Pleasure and delight at a job that's well done
Some gardens are providers for the table
Others grow different flowers as able

Design your outdoor space to please and suit you
Wonders of nature all around come what may
Somewhere maybe a creepy crawly or two
Birdsong is marvellous anytime of day
Colourful plants encourage insects it's true
Wonderment but attention you have to pay
The birds always busy flying here and there
Bird table or feed station to show you care

Children love rolling on a green grassy lawn
Happiness as they giggle and loudly shout
Joyful memories from the moment we're born
A perfect place to sit and relax no doubt
All things to all people it's never forlorn
Summertime some do get the barbecue out
Keep it tidy if this hobby you detest
Nature is wonderful and will do the rest.

Anne Sackey

WRITING A VILLANELLE LATE AT NIGHT

Late at night I like to get up to write
I never know what form my poem will take
But it has to be the villanelle tonight that's just right.

Each night suddenly the words come to light
And to the place where my pen and paper lie my way I make:
But it has to be the villanelle tonight that's just right.

Each night I do this before the words can take flight
As at this time my brain is active and wide awake:
Late at night I like to get up to write.

The outline of a poem is now in sight
Each night my thoughts are clear and not opaque:
But it has to be the villanelle tonight that's just right.

The words and lines have been quickly written down, each one of
them polite
In my boots there will be no need for me to quake:
Late at night I like to get up to write.

Each night what I write I hope will be to someone a delight
Now I've finished it's time for me to apply the brake:
Late at night I like to get up to write
But it has to be the villanelle tonight that's just right.

Patricia J Tausz

UNTITLED

I saw the man today, the man my friend spoke of.
There was I, sitting in the bus,
Laden with my usual shop, and the man passed.
Distinguished indeed, I turned round as my friend the owl does,
Eager to take in as much as I could possibly glean.
Tall he was, I thought might be a relic,
For indeed he had no infirmity, well... none visible.
Smart he was, his garb quite presentable,
I had heard that he gathered cigarette butts, and... his eyes,
Did cast a glare o'er the cig bin that sat outside the bus stop.
I was intrigued, certainly maketh a story,
The posh looking gent, with a strange hobby.
I'm excited to tell my friend, that indeed I have seen a stranger.
Smiling to myself, as the wee bus chugged away from the city,
I thought, *yes! I've seen the stranger,*
The stranger that is in town, with the strange, strange hobby.
Little things change my perspective on the world.
Little things... mean a lot.

Irene Gunnion

THE ERUPTION OF LIFE

Cold blue lava pouring mountain tremors
Flowing dripping sucked into volcanic inhalation
Fiery ice cracks red rock and blue liquid fuse in fury
The liquid adheres to dust and gravel
And the seeds of thousands of tiny waiting flowers
Delicately held in heavy mass of thick flowing lava
Foamy water spurts out of the ground
Whistling steam jets spit and hiss
Hot moisture ejected from deep within freezes and boils
And spatters in hot cold fusion
Air bubbles sinking breathing terraforming
New life buried under the earth
Waiting to be born in frothy flow
In chain reaction in lava rock earth air fire water
Spilling organisms into existence
From erupting geysers as cold meets hot meets red meets blue
And created in tumultuous amalgamation of the elements
Is the murky new beginning of what is to become bright and alive
And remembered not of ice fire and dirt and violent formation
But the sudden gush of clarity as life bursts open.

Christine King

BURY ST EDMUNDS

In the Abbey Gardens, we sit with our picnic in the shade.
The mass of pearl blue colour, is the ageratum blooming
with such delight.
Looking across at the outstanding beauty of what has been made.

A squirrel sits in a pouncing position on top of a pole,
at a good height.
People are sunbathing near the Abbey Ruins with pleasure.
We revisit this town remembering these amazing sights.

I take photographs of our lads which I will treasure.
Children are playing on the swings, some needing a helping hand.
It is lovely here, spending time of leisure.

Others are in the soft sand, a toddler is eating it,
thinking it's grand.
We must leave as more refreshments are required without delay.
In the courts, our boys play tennis,
the rules they try to understand.

At the Angel Hotel, baskets of petunias hang,
creating a lovely display.
In the town, there is a variety of shops
to investigate straight away.

Adrian Bullard

WHAT YOU DO TO ME

My heart flutters like the wing of a dove
Lifting my soul into a formation of love
Eros has ignited the hot flame of armour
His arrow has pierced my hearts inner core

Eager for you like a child on Christmas Eve
I pledge a vow only to you shall I cleave
Walking on air filled with the joys of spring
Beaming with glee, my heart begins to sing

Love is a drug, I'm constantly feeling high
Reverting to your image on my inward eye
I'm losing sleep and finding it hard to eat
Recalling the day you swept me off my feet

Even wild horses couldn't keep us apart
Your love was the key to unlocking my heart
My emotions tossed about as if on the breeze
Addicted to you like nectar to the bees

Special moments with you I will always savour
My undaunted love will never ever waiver
Like a love-sick puppy pining when you're gone
Our love will last forever, that you can count on.

Eva Lorraine Appleby

HELL

I'm battered by eternal hurricanes,
Internal, yet infernal. No one knows
And nor do I want to try to explain

Why I continue to endure these knocks and blows.
I'm calm amidst the pandemonium
And continue along the pathway that I chose

Presenting chilling equilibrium.
Inside, sins take place - murder, lust and rage,
Encased within my outer shell of tedium.

I hover between limbo and the stage
Where wild emotions spill: a river flowing.
But, like a Cardinal trapped within a cage

Flight is chained. Despite the tempest blowing
That would lift small wings, not see them brutally rent,
The oars are stilled, as Charon ceases rowing.

It should not be that my emotion's spent,
I want again to feel the fires of lust.
Familiarity beings sorrow without torment,
Ashes from the flames. My heart is dust.

Susan Cartwright-Smith

SWAMP RAP

Mob rule
We got mob rule

We got
Men in suits tellin' us lies
Ordinary people bein' burned alive
Brexit gangsters beatin' up on doctors
Deal or no deal talk all it does is mock us

Mob rule
We got mob rule

We got
Rural poverty no jobs no buses
Underfunded services with disappearin' nurses
Lies big and fat on the side of a train
Everyone treated like we got no brain

We got mob rule
We got mob rule

What we gonna do 'bout this travesty
Someone got to act not her majesty
Get ur face out ur phone
Please excuse my tone

But we got mob rule
We got mob rule

See with ur eyes
Hear with ur ears

Recognise the truth
Put aside fake fears

Or we got mob rule
We got mob rule

SWAMP - Sixtyish White Angry Mrs Poet.

Caroline Uwins

A LABOUR

She clamps
and calms
and cramps
in curiosity,

squeezing in
synchronicity
with my aching
vagueness,

her final grip:
an iron fist
forcing
my maternity.

Wringing out
her jam-filled
jail, she drips

like paint,
red - a shade
for love
and pain:

the colour
of me
and of my ambiguity:

a white
sheet
burgundy
with blood.

Maddened
muscles in
possession
of the divine,

the clench
of teeth in a
hardened neck
which scream

silently in
ripples down
my shattering
spine,

and as she
swims through
shrieking
bones,

echoic of my
youthful core,
her skin
my silhouette,

she leaves
my body
with my
soul.

Anna McNamara

BEATEN BY LOVE

Vows were voiced, the crowd rejoiced,
The day it all was said;
No doubtful qualms, each other's arms,
Held tight the day they wed.

An easy fit, the rings did sit,
Well chosen with their love;
A future bright by candlelight,
Romantic as a dove.

A crack appeared, a word she feared,
When harshly it was spoken;
The bubble popped, the kindness stopped,
Tears fell and hearts were broken.

She did not choose to be bruised,
His hand hit hard at times;
The candle flame began to wane,
As actions crossed the lines.

She forgave, the bloody wave,
That brought her to her knees;
To dominate with bitter hate,
Innate was this disease.

It broke her heart for them to part,
Privately she cried;
The beatings cold, her spirit sold,
As all the love had died.

Christine Carol Burrows

ALIENATION

The people around me, it seems,
Speak a language not my own.
Their words - muffled
Their thoughts - scattered
Their signals not quite caught.
Their words are obscure
Or just faint, muffled sounds, I guess.
As though their frequency does not fall within my range.
Is it higher or lower than I can hear?
I don't know.
I find it abnormal.
Their philosophies, beyond my ability to assimilate;
A massive difference in the strength of mentality
Great difference in the level of intellect.
Theirs higher,
Or mine?
I don't know.
Our ideas hardly intersect.
The attitude towards life - parallel!
The eccentricity
The alienation is frustrating.
Choking.
It corrodes me.
Am I the only normal in the abnormal world
Or the abnormal in a normal world?
I don't know.

Delores James

MY FATHER

For all my life,
You have made me feel alive,
Taught me right from wrong,
Cherished me throughout my
Life and guided me along.

As a father, you have cared,
For me,
Spared me from any harm,
I appreciate all that you do,
I love you.

There comes a time,
When we have had a mountain
To climb,
But we have seen that the
Grass is greener on the other side.

However hard it has been,
We have made a new life
For ourselves,
We are all happier now
And are seen to be stronger than ever.

Even though we have had
Our ups and downs,
We are still as solid
As a rock,
Whatever happens nothing
Will ever take that away.

Right now we have
To think about the
Most important thing
In life and that is you.

I love you.

Sarah-Jayne Hunter

REGRET

While the sun and moon danced overhead
We came together one summer's day;
But I don't remember what you said.

We walked beside the river bed,
Our words tumbling over the spillway.
While the sun and moon danced overhead

I took your shy hand and gently spread
Your fingers around a blossom spray,
But I don't remember what you said.

I looked into your eyes filled with dread
And knew your heart's song was lost that day,
While the sun and moon danced overhead.

I saw your bright soul had been misled
Confused by what you might never say.
But I don't remember what you said.

Now the day slips away, a regret?
I chose to forget our yesterday.
As the sun and moon dance overhead,
Only now, do I recall what you said.

Andrew Elze

I'M

I'm heartbroken, I'm sad
Sometimes I'm just plain lazy
Occasionally I'll admit I am glad
But for the most part, I'm totally crazy

I'm tinged with sorrow; reality is hazy
There's a storm brewing in my teacup
The forecast's cloudy and rainy
I'm totally fed up

I'm elated, I'm deflated; I'm bang out of luck
I'm downtrodden and forgotten, I am filled with hatred
I'm sorry and I'm worried that nobody gives a fuck
I'm overwhelmed and overlooked, I'm utterly devastated

I'm a wicked old witch, I'm a big bad bitch, I'm heavily sedated
I'm unstable and unable; I am hopping mad
I'm addicted and restricted
I am really, really sad

Anna Tregidgo

THE DEVIL'S CRY

The legends so to speak hidden
Amongst the shallow sheep that sigh,
A devil and an angel meet fiercely
Amongst the fire, the great fire
Opprest the wicked thy rest
The angel smirks with the devilish smile
From the Devil's eye there is a cry
O' God I am innocent I confess
The angel is neither good nor best
She is in fact a traitor. To the heart of his land
The judges of high court come to demand
And speak with linguine tongue
I find the defendant of the angel guilty
As obliged, the angel smirked but this time
The Devil met his fate, from an empty window
Stood a wicked transparent lake
It was there only there would the Devil be free
And the angel is sentenced to death.

Leanne Drain

VIRTUES AND VICES

Your virtues made me love you.
Your vices made me hate you.

Your virtues are shown to all.
Your vices are hidden and small.

Small they may be, but deadly they are.
Your vices are what left the scar

on my chest, straight above my heart.
Your vices are what prevent me to start

loving another, in fear he has the same
vices, that'll only taint my name

even further, as damaged, as wrecked, as unloved.
Your vices are forever going to come

and haunt me under the guise of your virtues.
I'm overjoyed when you bring me brilliant news

that you've left her; and you can now be with me.
But it was your vices that finally set you free.

Sarina Kiayani

PRIDE

You're selling your soul to the Devil,
That deadly sin will twist your heart,
Your hate is hitting another level,
That hurt will tear your world apart.

You need to stop and think this through
You're crossing a bridge that leads nowhere,
In your heart you know this isn't you,
Your life consumed by your own despair.

Nodding dogs praise your way,
You listen to their encouraging yap,
Bitter is the way you'll always stay,
Don't fall into their awaiting trap.

Hate isn't a place you want to live,
Look through the clouds and see the sun,
Move on and let your head forgive,
Before it ends a life that's barely begun.

Lisa Wileman

PHONICS (A SAPPHIC ODE)

When the day is drawing to its conclusion,
And the Kansas-grey of the afternoon seeps
Through the sun-scorched panes of the first floor window,
You are in colour:

Dusky half-light brushes across your skin and
Gilds it softly, whispering all the hopes of
Summer in your ear. I can see the remnants
Of frost fall back,

Leaving you, exposed as a newborn infant,
Virgin snow where children have not yet tread, an
Unfilled diary, waiting for ink's caress. A
Sapling. A nymph.

Fine-spun words are trickling from your mouth, and
Every single consonant sends a shiver,
Like a droplet, bruising my spine. Your vowel sounds
Render me spellbound.

Hannah Bradburn

OF THE LANDSCAPE NEAR THE RIVER URE

(A sonnet)

Lofty boughs line the rolling banks,
Slow breeze rolling over the meadow.
Light dances upon the gentle flow,
Alert deer roam through the oaken ranks.

Gentle sun reflects on a scene so serene,
Chirping birds whose sound echoes around.
Through the landscape the river flows winding, between
Fair hills, meadow, copse, plain and mound.

For such beauty was by ages developed,
As life which likewise follows in parallel the course.
Unrivalled beauty which should never be enveloped,
Lives then twist and turn from beginning at source.

Some are great, some are small, but all smart and finish the same,
Meanders, rapids and tributaries, become our name.

Alexander Walsh

LOVE AFTER DEATH

Three lands formed the afterlife;
Heaven was the land of morals and order,
Hell was the land of wickedness and chaos,
Limbo, very much like Earth - blended both.

Heaven is full of infants
And Satan's quite a nice chap.
Michael Jackson's been elected as President
Beating Adolf Hitler once again.

I lost my head in the prologue of summer.
I met my lost boys and golden age daughter.
My husband had some other wives before he died.
He found that other roses were sweeter than mine.

Henry had a harem.
Elizabeth had an army.
My boys had their little wings.
I had Richard III: underneath his clothes.

Chloe Gilholy

MAGIC IN OUR LAND

(A garland cinquain)

Fairies
Do not forget
Don't take a second guess
At what one might well be thinking
Take heed

Goblins
See in our world
Something mischievous
In ways, we do not comprehend
Take note

Pixies
Not of this time
Absolute enchantment
Complex creature with complex minds
Take care

Brownies
See our planet
As we all should see it
A wonderland of pure delight
Take joy

Spirits
Nothing is weird
Do not be so fearful
All exist in different realms
Take ease

Fairies
See in our world
Absolute enchantment
A wonderland of pure delight
Take heed.

Lee Montgomery-Hughes

SEASONAL SONNET

You asked me, "What's your favourite season?"
I replied, "It's impossible to say."
You'll think it odd, without rhyme or reason,
I can't choose between December and May.
Daffodils, new life and lengthening days.
Summer sun, silver sand, foaming white seas.
Leaves falling, birds calling, flying away.
Diamond bright snow on the branches of trees.
I cannot name my favourite season,
I'm finding it impossible to say.
I know it's odd, without rhyme or reason,
Not to choose between December and May.
Each season leaves memories in its wake,
That's why this choice is hard for me to make.

Mary Chapman

WANDERING CHILD

It is when we find ourselves
at that very darkest time in life.
When everything we try to do
seems to turn against us -
and every new road we travel,
leads to another dead end.
When it seems our prayers
all go unanswered.

This is the very moment -
when the clouds will part.
A voice will speak,
through the mind of Man -

"My wandering child,
did you really think I had forsaken you?
The roads you had chosen to follow
would have taken you into bitter despair.
It was I, who gently guided you back.

I am the light -
in your darkest hour.
I shine, for all eternity."

Nina Graham

PRAISE

Worthy is Him who sits upon the throne.
Worthy is the lamb more precious than rings.
Sing songs of praise to the king of all kings.
The lamb of God who is the cornerstone
He was slain for us so we're not alone.
Receiving honour to Heaven He brings.
God's wealth and power stretch beyond all things.
Great is His name on Heaven and earth known.
Lamb of God who was slain for me and you.
Praise and glory to His wonderful name
So much His wisdom and power can do.
The lamb receives honour without the shame.
There's enough strength and wealth He can use too.
God's wealth and wisdom are greater than fame.

Nicola Penistone

I DROOL FOR THEE

The box is warm and holds my joy within;
You turn up late but I am barely fussed;
The smell that wafts out yellows me in sin;
A soul condemned with sight of golden crust.
Your perfect layers steaming gently there,
With softest dough, the wondrous sauce and cheese,
Combined to send your scent into the air,
And bring me down to worship on my knees.
I hold your flopping form in practised grip.
I bite your end and groan in greasy glee.
I dunk your crust in smooth and sour dip,
Then wipe the plate until it's sparkling clean.
But now I'm full and vow to curse your name,
Until I make that fateful call again.

Harry Husbands

IN PRAISE OF CONTENTMENT

The child sees life as just a game to play
What's sweet is right, all else forever wrong
But childhood dreams are ended in a day
And innocence becomes a bitter song.

Man strives to gain the eagle's dizzy height
He sneers at those who choose the middle way
All he seeks in life is love and light
But finds that joy is kin to cold dismay.

The old man knows the colours of the fool
And grey fits the ambitions of the old
Perhaps and maybe now impose their rule
And doubt becomes the ruler of the bold.

Young or old we seek what isn't there
But in the end content defeats despair.

John Plevin

SMOKING IN THE ROSES

Smoke blown across you scent,
Expensive drift into rose petals on necks,
You greet with kiss of angel, made to join,
Our freckles sprinkled on each other,
We intimate, circled in arms.

Take a hair from your brow,
Store it in blue box near my bed,
Kept to remind me we must be wed,
Not bitter love and better we keep now,
Our intentions fated in thought.
Swallow each other's words, hold rings and ribbons,
Sing at morning like spring birds, returning,
Married in mind, coloured plants in hands,
As light in fog and in memory, songs to sing,
We are elated at altar, know lives are intertwined.

Alan Gardner

KATHERINE BAXTER, LADY OF THE MAP II

There is a friend we'd like you to know
Bright as the sun with her golden glow
Come all ye nations, please come and see
Our mate, it's Katherine B:

Katherine Baxter, lady of the map!
Katherine Baxter, lady of the map!
Please just be patient and you will see
She'll draw a map for thee.

It's in her feather, it's in her cap
New York and London into a map
Near to the river, where she abides
Free from the rising tides;

Sent her by God to preach here today
We are intrigued by what she will say
With ink and graphite in one accord
Drawing the Holy Word.

John Oludotun Showemimo

A SONNET FOR THE GARDEN

Hazelnut ties form the brown canopy,
Dirt from the earth gives a bed to the plants;
Ensuing girl passing through white, soppy,
Flies unknown to the naked eye like chants;
Of celestial nectar brought to fill a cup,
Pine grove smothers the lily groves today;
Evergreen spring tides fantasy's pre-nup,
Seeds implanted from the undergrowth of clay;
Volcanic ashes give moss a new life,
To spur from nothing to see everything,
In a garden of green viewed from Fife,
A tilt of the head backwards arrests a fling;
Sensations produce ideas that thaw feeling,
The age old conquest of time has no ceiling.

Liba Ravindran

SUNRISE

(A sonnet)

The morning breaks without the heat of day,
The silence of the night that breathless kissed
Spreads thin across the air, in rippled sway,
And tumbles down into a sobering mist.
The covers slowly pull back and reveal
The softly humming dawn, now perched with tears
Upon a dozing trunk where every peel
Of life climbs up to ease her tender fears.
And I approached my sobbing lover's side
And loved her all the more for such a sting,
I cast away the nightly glittering pride
To comfort all that's ever comforting.
And now the sun has risen in the sky
How happy is the woven heart to die!

Joseph G Lay

BLINDLY IN LOVE

Oh my love tell me you'll come near,
The word prescribes you for me,
Sing a song only I can hear,
You've got my heart now throw away the key.

Your hair is worthy of several caresses,
I can sense you through my touch,
I've never been one to make guesses,
They say I'm accurate and such.

Allow me to linger a kiss or two,
Perhaps you'll grant me more,
Let me taste the air that serves you,
You must want me... I... I am sure.

But you had to realise I was devoid of vision,
And now you have broken me with your decision.

Nishita Choudhury

RIGOLETTO'S DEMISE IN TERZA RIMA

I long to see the theatre's strident sign
I long to feel the thrill and lust and pain
I long to watch the set and drink and dine
I long to bear the fast and driving rain
I long for fame and fortune on my way
And feel so small, unable to attain
I long for chance, to shout and beat them all
As my bus stops I hesitantly trot
To shout out Rigoletto's opera call
Yet not to pull the strings or make them fall
His reputation no more than a sot?
A romantic lethal plot which so appals?
Proving the scene was pulling in a dime
I long to see theatrical in crime.

Tracy Allott

SPECIAL NIGHT

Suddenly there was a real rainy night
I could not believe it, was I dreaming?
The window revealed rain in plain sight
What was my brain, in beauty, becoming?
Was it mingling with rainwater on pears?
Was it flying overhead, not clouding?
Certainly I felt not sad grievous tears
I heard the music of rainfall chiming
I was amazed at that sudden rainfall
I counted seconds while it was streaming
I began, at that time, to love it all
The Earth, the sky, and all of Earth's beings
After many dry nights, sudden downpour
I flung open all my windows and doors.

Muhammad Khurram Salim

BUTTERFLY

I am waiting for her in the summer park,
a contented couple with ice creams saunter past
jealousy rearing its hideous head.
It is then that the beauty of the day
appears in all its majesty:
under a cobalt Dali painting sky
my eyes view a flickering butterfly,

a Red Admiral with hues
as rich as the irises, roses, forget-me-nots
patrols the flower bed together with a bee,
entrancing transience, grace and beauty.
My phone rings, she will not be coming
and now the butterfly has flown away
as the trees hiss on this warm summer's day.

Guy Fletcher

MEAN GIRLS

For all the broken sleep, awkward encounters and no replies
Not a fair exchange, for all the hurt, anger and lies
Wracking yourself with guilt, for something you don't feel is worth fixing
All for a friendship you haven't even been missing
It lacked support, interaction and worse an interest from both sides
Any smart person would choose to cut the ties
The lack of communication did hinder
Only for them to listen to a Chinese whisper
Not even enough faith to ask another opinion

Well it's no surprise from a queen bee's minion

Geraldine Tunstall

LOVE IS THE ESSENCE

Love is the essence of life
Only with love we can overcome the strife
It's not created by man-made rules
Those who place barriers are the fools

Too many people have no love in their heart
Without this fundamental force, they would fall apart
How can you love with your heart's true desire?
When you place boundaries, true love you'll never acquire

Love is a solution to problems we face
For it to manifest requires time and space
Give love a try, it gives love a chance
Pray to the Lord above and receive romance

Jeevan Sagoo

UNTITLED

There once was a man called Snow,
If the White Walkers came he would know.
He wore a black coat,
Northern he spoke.
Now to The Wall he must go.

There was a tough girl from Sunnydale,
In slaying vampires she would prevail.
She fought demons as well,
They went straight to Hell.
Their complexion was always quite pale.

Here is a man who is the nation's saviour,
He speaks of the earth and animal behaviours.
He is engaging and kind,
His voice is sublime.
His narration on life we all favour.

Stephanie Dodsworth

LOVE MAKES YOU OR BREAKS YOU

Love is like an open book
No one can understand it, it is far more complex than it seems,
But sometimes all it takes is one look
To start something exciting and new
An adventure that leaves you breathless
Makes you feel alive by letting you fly
But other times it can leave you broken-hearted and deathless
Some say it's better to love than not love at all
But the truth is love does hurt you
Sometimes
Leaving you pale and blue
The choice is yours, will you fall?
Will you rise?
Or, will you break all ties?

Anisa Begum

CLOWNS

(A rondeau)

What lies behind a painted smile?
Let us tarry for a short while.
A clown's life is an empty one,
Each day must be seen having fun
Clowns dress in a colourful style.

They make memories people file,
While worries create inner bile
But cannot be seen looking glum.
What lies behind...

Removed from all real life awhile,
Perform tricks - comedic pile,
Clowns are like us, when said and done,
For they have a dad and a mum.
Is there a helpline they can dial?
What lies behind...

Sue Mullinger

MY LOVE

My love is not a fool
My love is cool
My love is chill
My love always will be there
Any time, any place, anywhere
As my love is pure
That's for sure
My love is strong
And it won't go wrong
My love loves to see you smile
Even, if it is for a short while
My heart beats a million times for you
For this heart of mine is really true
My love, I love to hear your voice
It always makes me rejoice
Every time you walk by
So, my love never says goodbye.

Yvette Avonda Layne

SHE

And yet I find
on looking round
there's nought to see
that once was me
no memory
however kind
can I be sure
which way to go
the night is dark
no light or spark
my heart this part
alone is pure
and free from sin
which I knew well
all Satan's ways
I spent my days
so in a daze
so far from Him
the lonely years
till she came by
she took my hand
she understands
God's promised land
a time for tear.

Robert Stevens

STORM

It started with a little cloud
Growing dark and anvil form,
The air a stifling, throttling shroud
Chokes the usual sunny norm.
The drip, drip, drop of a little shower
Grows heavy and hurtful, sad,
Drowning, sinking, full of power
Now a torrent running mad.
Thunderous racket, dreadful rumble,
Sparks from high ignite.
The world around begins to tumble,
A fearsome, awful sight.
But once more it's over fast,
One more fight not set to last.

George McDermid

FIVE BATS

At dusk,
Screaming louder
than you can hear; dancers,
Jauntily in the air, catching
insects.

You will
see-not-see us
flying, sounding out prey.
Food for furry tummy eats, treats.
Tasty.

Back at
our habitats,
We hang out together,
Chatting though tired; upside down
sleeping.

Look out
for us with care,
We will be there flying.
We're elegant, we're beautiful,
We're bats.

James Corah

TOGETHER!

To those that showed care,
Together we'll make the world fair.
To those that believed,
Together we'll create honesty.
To those that showed me the way,
Together we'll have our say.
To those that were by my side,
Together we'll prevent a divide.
To those that were kind,
Together we'll bind.
To that showed love,
Together we'll fly above.
To those that were fair,
Together we'll show the world that we care!

Bushra Latif

YOUR LOST LOVE

Whenever you lose the one you love
Your heart feels so lonely and sad
For they were the best and sometimes only friend
That you'll ever have had
For they'll try to make you happy
Should you ever feel sad
And they'll always walk by your side
Whenever times get bad
So hold on tight and never forget
Those good and happy memories you now hold
In your heart
And the ones you have loved and lost
Will walk by your side forever

Donald John Tye

CORMORANT

Cormorant, perching on a post so gallant,
Black wings in prowess outstretched, regal, valiant.
Dives like a bow fired arrow
Into the ocean blue,
Hunting, skewering fish
To gulp, swallow with a chew
Where there is no sorrow.
Then for a bobbing paddle,
With a wing tail wiggle and waggle,
Hopped onto a boat clawed webbed feet
In a happy dancing shanty pitter-patter
Flying off leaving an oily feather shaked paddle.

Keith William Newing

UNTIL WE MEET AGAIN

(An Epistle)

I used to wait for you,
The same time and place every day
I'm sure you remember?
Then that last time you never came
And I knew then
That I would have to learn to live without you
Although we will always have our memories
Of happier times spent together.
And the love that shaped me into this strong confident person
Enabled by your love to follow this path alone
Until we meet again, my love.

Paula Holdstock

STRUGGLE

I'm thinking so hard, my thoughts all hidden.
It feels like they're locked up and forbidden.
I just want to unlock them with a key.
I just want them to be free!
But, they are ever so slow to release...
My pen and notepad are ready to scribble down a poem or song.
But, my thoughts are taking far too long!
I'm unsure of what to write,
The sun is no longer bright.
This is a struggle!

Rani Latif

AN ASPECT OF FREEDOM

6 o'clock am.

Like snow on the mountain tops,
early morning sun
glinted on the dark clouds
gathering in force
for the downpour,
forecast on radio.

Just like the snow
on the mountain tops
as the sun rose higher
in the leaden sky,
the 'mountain top' clouds
lost their sun-snow.

The dark clouds dispersed.
It did not rain!

Pearl Foy-Stubley

OTTAVA RIMA

After love is gone, what is left for me?
When pastures new seem barren as the dust,
I'm left to write my lines of prosody,
whilst interludes I have leave me non-plussed.
Oh compass of emotions help me see,
the path I take and who on earth to trust,
regret is such a waste of mental space,
I look for something which I can't replace.

Nelson Brooks

DECREASING CIRCLES

Looking at you from afar,
As you deal with your
Ever decreasing circles,
Who do you turn to when you are
Managing mere mortals.

Dusk turns into dark
Everything must come to pass
Now we all wait for miracles
And you deal with your
Ever decreasing circles.

Karthik Subramanya

COMING OUT

I want to come out.
Hold me tight till I can stand
Alone in the light
And shine!

Flickering in shadow,
Unsteady and slight,
Uncertain, unsure
To love or fight?

Will it hurt?
Will I be alright?
Will I die?
Can I breathe in the light?

Jacinta Mcshane

WINTER FIELD

Sheep stand,
Heads lowered
Over the stunted
Seasonal verdure,
In the standard grazing pose;
Facing the same
Bordering fence,
Like model farm animals
Set in place
By a meticulous child;
Flanks daubed
With the cold gold
Of the settling sun

David Burl

DISORDER

Deep,
Darkened
Crevices
Where none can rest,
Functioning only
To exist—but not live.
They spend their lives in shadow,
Without the hope we all should feel—
Destined to a state of misery,
All motivation gone and never free.

Jean Aked

MY WIFE

Come walk with me my darling
Down Memory Lane
Where everything is different yet
everything's the same
We have always been together
We have never been apart
We have always loved each other
Right from the very start

Robin Morgan

BUTTERFLY DREAMS

(Butterfly cinquain)

Fair nymph.
Sweet butterfly.
Drink of life's nectar, sweet.
Delicate wings that catch the sun.
And move.
To tease my dull, saddened senses.
Lift my drooping spirit.
Fly to my heart.
Fair nymph.

Margaret Edge

MOTHER'S EGG

(In memory of my mum)

Our love was strong like an egg
Once it was broken life was never the same
Because one cannot live without the other
My heart is broken
And one day the egg will be complete
When we are together again.

George Fisher

TWO ABREAST

There was a young lady from Oldham
Who said, "Would you like to hold 'em?"
I said, "If I could
Forever I would,
I'll just get some plaster and mould 'em."

Tom Higgins

OVERFLOWING RAIN

A gentle pitter-patter from the yard outside
A most delicious splatter all in all.
My forehead on the window just to stare entranced
As overflow cascading makes a drizzly dance.

Gareth McLaughlin

HUMAN, NATURE

(A tanka)

A stomach crunches,
like vine twisting within wall.
Muscles ache and pang,
as tree trunks groan in winter.
Human, nature: both know pain.

Thomas Harrison

MEG

I have a sister called Meg
One day she broke her leg
She fell in a puddle
I gave her a cuddle
But she stank like a rotten egg

Doris K Williams

HAIKU FOR JULY

Nothing exotic
Can quite match the surprise when
England's summer works.

Christopher Sleeman

UNTITLED

(A haiku)

Moonbeams were jewels
In her hair, I was dazzled
Spellbound by lost love.

Nigel Pearce

HAIKU

alone sea watching
white wave sweeps in and leaves a
shining pebble gift

P J Reed

FORWARD POETRY
INFORMATION

We hope you have enjoyed reading this book - and that you will continue to enjoy it in the coming years.

For free poetry workshops please visit **www.forwardpoetry.co.uk**. Here you can also subscribe to our monthly newsletter.

Alternatively, If you would like to order further copies of this book or any of our other titles, then please give us a call or log onto our website.

Forward Poetry Information
Remus House
Coltsfoot Drive
Peterborough
PE2 9BF

(01733) 890099